Diabetic for Beginners

Great-Tasting Recipes to Help You Balance your Blood Sugars

Crystal Ashby

work can be in any fashion deemed liable for any hardship or damages that may befall them after undertaking information described herein.

Additionally, the information in the following pages is intended only for informational purposes and should thus be thought of as universal. As befitting its nature, it is presented without assurance regarding its prolonged validity or interim quality. Trademarks that are mentioned are done without written consent and can in no way be considered an endorsement from the trademark holder.

TABLE OF CONTENTS

Introduction

Diabetes is a condition where the body is no longer able to self-regulate blood glucose. When you eat food containing carbs (coming from honey, apples, or brown rice), your body breaks it down into glucose during digestion. This one passes into the blood through the walls of the intestines, which causes blood sugar to rise.

In reply, the pancreas secretes a hormone called "Insulin." Its role is to lower the blood sugar back to normal levels by moving the sugar out of the blood and into the cells, used for energy. But if you are a diabetic the blood sugar builds up in the bloodstream, resulting in high blood sugar.

A diabetes diagnosis means that the pancreas is not able to produce enough insulin to keep up with this resistance, and then insulin deficiency is the result. If your body can't make enough insulin, blood sugar levels become elevated.

Long-term elevated blood sugar levels can affect almost every system in the body; health complications as heart disease, stroke, kidney failure, nerve damage, eye damage, and blindness.

There are plenty of foods that will improve your symptoms and make your life easier:

- ✓ Whole grains.
- ✓ Low-carb tubers and roots. Fresh, frozen, or raw vegetables.
- ✓ Fresh fruit with high-fiber content.
- ✓ Sugar-free and calorie-free products.
- ✓ Freshly boiled beans.
- ✓ Nuts and seeds.
- ✓ Fresh meat.
- ✓ Whole dairy.
- ✓ Black coffee.

Diabetic Recipes

Egg Cups

Time required:
20 minutes

Servings: 12

INGREDIENTS

10 Eggs, large

½ tsp. Black Pepper

1 ½ tsp. Salt

¾ tsp. Italian
Seasoning

¾ cup Parmesan
Cheese, grated

½ tsp. Garlic Powder

1 cup Spinach,
chopped

1 cup Tomatoes, ripe
and chopped

¾ cup Ham, cooked
and chopped,
optional

STEPS FOR COOKING

1. Preheat the oven to 400° F.
2. Crack the eggs into a large mixing bowl and spoon in salt and pepper.
3. Whisk the mixture well with a whisker.
4. Once combined, stir in garlic powder and Italian seasoning. Mix well and then add spinach, tomato, and cheese. Use ham if needed. Combine.
5. Pour the mixture into greased muffin pans lined with silicone liners.
6. Fill 2/3rd of the cups and add more cheese if desired.
7. Finally, bake them for 13 to 15 minutes or until set.
8. Serve and enjoy.

Whole-Grain Dutch Baby Pancake

Time required:
30 minutes

Servings: 04

INGREDIENTS

2 tablespoons coconut oil

1/2 cup whole-wheat flour

¼ cup skim milk 3 large eggs

1 teaspoon vanilla extract

1/2 teaspoon baking powder

¼ teaspoon salt

¼ teaspoon ground cinnamon

Powdered sugar, for dusting

STEPS FOR COOKING

1. Preheat the oven to 400f.
2. Put the coconut oil in a medium oven-safe skillet, and place the skillet in the oven to melt the oil while it preheats.
3. In a blender, combine the flour, milk, eggs, vanilla, baking powder, salt, and cinnamon. Process until smooth.
4. Carefully remove the skillet from the oven and tilt to spread the oil around evenly.
5. Pour the batter into the skillet and return it to the oven for 23 to 25 minutes, until the pancake puffs and lightly browns.
6. Remove, dust lightly with powdered sugar, cut into 4 wedges, and serve.

Apple Filled Swedish Pancake

Time required:
45 minutes

Servings: 06

INGREDIENTS

2 apples, cored and sliced thin

¾ cup egg substitute

½ cup fat-free milk

½ cup sugar-free caramel sauce

1 tbsp. reduced-calorie margarine

½ cup flour

1–1/2 tbsp. brown sugar substitute

2 tsp. water

¼ tsp. cinnamon

1/8 tsp. cloves

1/8 tsp. salt

Non-stick cooking spray

STEPS FOR COOKING

1. Heat the oven to 400°F. Place the margarine in the cast iron or oven-proof skillet, and place it in the oven until the margarine is melted.

2. In a medium bowl, whisk together flour, milk, egg substitute, cinnamon, cloves, and salt until smooth.

3. Pour the batter into a hot skillet and bake 20–25 minutes until puffed and golden brown.

4. Spray a medium saucepan with cooking spray. Heat over medium heat.

5. Add apples, brown sugar, and water. Cook, stirring occasionally until apples are tender and golden brown, about 4–6 minutes.

INGREDIENTS	STEPS FOR COOKING
	6. Pour the caramel sauce into a microwave-proof measuring glass and heat 30–45 seconds, or until warmed through.
	7. To serve, spoon apples into pancake and drizzle with caramel. Cut into wedges.

Coleslaw with Lime

Time required:
15 minutes

Servings: 04

INGREDIENTS

1 teaspoon of Salt

1/4 cup of Water

1 clove of Garlic

2 tablespoons of lime juice

1/4 cup fresh coriander leaves

2 avocados

400 g of ready-made coleslaw

STEPS FOR COOKING

1. Chop the cilantro and garlic and put them in a blender along with a little bit of water, add the 2 avocados + lime juice and blend until creamy.

2. Mix the ready-made coleslaw with the dressing you just made and toss well.

3. Enjoy your meal!

Bagels

Time required:
30 minutes

Servings: 06

INGREDIENTS	STEPS FOR COOKING

INGREDIENTS

1 tbsp. Baking Powder

1 ½ cup Almond Flour blanched

2 Eggs, large and beaten

2 ½ cup Mozzarella Cheese, shredded

2 oz. Cream Cheese, cubed

STEPS FOR COOKING

1. Preheat the oven to 400° F.
2. Combine almond flour and baking powder in a mixing bowl. Set aside.
3. Mix the mozzarella cheese and cream cheese in a large microwave-safe bowl and heat it for 2 minutes on high power. Stir halfway through and at the end.
4. Add the flour mixture and eggs to the cheese mixture and make a dough out of it by kneading it quickly.
5. As the dough will be sticky, keep kneading it until it becomes smooth. Tip: If the dough seems too difficult to mix or is still sticky, you can microwave it again for another 15 to 20 seconds to make it soften.

INGREDIENTS	STEPS FOR COOKING
	6. Divide the dough into six portions and roll it into a long log.
	7. Press the ends together of the long log to get the bagel shape. Arrange them on a parchment paper-lined baking sheet.
	8. Finally, bake them for 12 to 14 minutes or until the bagels are firm and golden in color.

Mushroom, Zucchini, and Onion Frittata

Time required: 30 minutes

Servings: 04

INGREDIENTS

1 tablespoon extra-virgin olive oil

1/2 onion, chopped

1 medium zucchini, chopped

1 1/2 cups sliced mushrooms

6 large eggs, beaten

2 tablespoons skim milk

Salt

Freshly ground black pepper

1-ounce feta cheese, crumbled

STEPS FOR COOKING

1. Preheat the oven to 400 F.
2. In an oven-safe skillet over medium-high heat, heat the olive oil.
3. Add the onion, then sauté for 3 to 5 minutes, until translucent.
4. Add the zucchini and mushrooms, and cook for 3 to 5 more minutes, until the vegetables are tender.
5. Meanwhile, in a small bowl, whisk the eggs, milk, salt, and pepper. Pour the mixture into the skillet, stirring to combine, and transfer the skillet to the oven. Cook for 7 to 9 minutes, until set.

6. Sprinkle with the feta cheese, and cook for 1 to 2 minutes more, until heated through.
7. Remove, cut into 4 wedges, and serve.

Breakfast Pizza

Time required:
40 minutes

Servings: 08

INGREDIENTS	STEPS FOR COOKING

INGREDIENTS

12 eggs

½ lb. breakfast sausage

1 cup bell pepper, sliced

1 cup red pepper, sliced

1 cup cheddar cheese, grated

½ cup half-and-half

½ tsp. salt

¼ tsp. pepper

STEPS FOR COOKING

1. Heat oven to 350°F.
2. In a large cast-iron skillet, brown the sausage. Transfer to a bowl.
3. Add peppers and cook for 3–5 minutes or until they begin to soften. Transfer to a bowl.
4. In a small bowl, whisk together the eggs, cream, salt, and pepper. Pour into the skillet. Cook for 5 minutes or until the sides start to set.
5. Bake for 15 minutes.
6. Remove from the oven and set it to broil. Top "crust" with sausage, peppers, and cheese. Broil for 3 minutes, or until cheese is melted and starts to brown.
7. Let rest for 5 minutes before slicing and serving.

Oatmeal Fondant

Time required:
5 minutes

Servings: 01

INGREDIENTS

1/3 cup coconut milk

1/2 cup hemp seeds

1 tablespoon melted butter

1 tablespoon Chia seeds

3 tablespoons cocoa powder

3 drops liquid Stevia

½ teaspoon of vanilla extract

A pinch of Himalayan salt

STEPS FOR COOKING

1. Combine all ingredients in a jar and mix well until evenly blended.
2. Refrigerate the mixture and let it sit overnight.
3. Enjoy your meal!

Waffles

Time required:
20 minutes

Servings: 02

INGREDIENTS	STEPS FOR COOKING

INGREDIENTS

½ cup Almond Flour, blanched

¼ cup Almond Milk, unsweetened

1 Egg, large and separated

2 tbsp. Butter

2 tbsp. Erythritol

½ tsp. Vanilla Extract

½ tsp. Baking Powder

2 tbsp. Nut Butter of your choice

¼ tsp. Sea Salt

STEPS FOR COOKING

1. Preheat the waffle iron to high heat and grease it with oil.
2. Crack the egg into a bowl and whisk it until you get stiff peaks.
3. Mix almond flour, salt, erythritol, and baking powder in another bowl. Keep aside.
4. Melt butter and nut butter in a microwave-safe bowl.
5. Spoon this butter mixture into the flour mixture. Combine.
6. Once combined, stir in egg yolk, vanilla essence, and almond milk to it and give everything a good stir until you get a smooth mixture.
7. Fold the egg whites gently into the batter so that you get a fluffy and light mixture.

8. Pour half the batter into the waffle iron and close. Cook for 5 minutes or until the steam stops coming. Repeat with the remaining batter.

9. Serve and enjoy.

Lovely Porridge

Time required:
15 minutes

Servings: 02

INGREDIENTS

2 tablespoons
coconut flour

2 tablespoons
vanilla protein
powder

3 tablespoons
Golden Flaxseed
meal

1 and 1/2 cups
almond milk,
unsweetened

powdered erythritol

STEPS FOR COOKING

1. Take a bowl and mix in flaxseed meal, protein powder, coconut flour and mix well

2. Add mix to the saucepan (placed over medium heat)

3. Add almond milk and stir, let the mixture thicken

4. Add your desired amount of sweetener and serve

5. Enjoy!

Almond Flour Porridge

Time required:
10 minutes

Servings: 01

INGREDIENTS

1 tsp. Erythritol, granulated

2 tbsp. Flaxseed, grounded

½ cup Almond Milk, unsweetened

2 tbsp. Almond Flour

2 tbsp. Sesame Seeds, grounded

STEPS FOR COOKING

1. Combine the sesame seeds, flaxseed meal, and almond flour in a microwave-safe bowl and mix well.
2. To this, pour the almond milk and heat it on high power for one minute in the microwave.
3. Stir in the mixture and heat it again for one minute. Add more milk if the mixture seems thicker.
4. Sprinkle the erythritol over it and combine it.

Basil and Tomato Baked Eggs

Time required:
25 minutes

Servings: 04

INGREDIENTS

1 garlic clove,
minced

1 cup canned
tomatoes

¼ cup fresh basil
leaves, roughly
chopped

1/2 teaspoon chili
powder

1 tablespoon olive
oil

4 whole eggs

Salt and pepper to
taste

STEPS FOR COOKING

1. Preheat your oven to 375 degrees F.
2. Take a small baking dish and grease it with olive oil.
3. Add garlic, basil, tomatoes chili, olive oil into a dish, then stir.
4. Crackdown eggs into a dish, keeping space between the two, then sprinkle the whole dish with salt and pepper.
5. Place in oven and cook for 12 minutes until eggs are set and tomatoes are bubbling.
6. Serve with basil on top.
7. Enjoy!

Avocado Fries

Time required:
30 minutes

Servings: 02

INGREDIENTS

1 medium avocado, pitted

1 egg

1/2 cup almond flour

¼ tsp. ground black pepper

1/2 tsp. salt

2 tsp. olive oil

STEPS FOR COOKING

1. Switch on the air fryer, insert fryer basket, grease it with olive oil, then shut with its lid, set the fryer at 400°F, and preheat for 10 minutes.

2. Meanwhile, cut the avocado in half and then cut each half into wedges, each about ½-inch thick.

3. Place flour in a shallow dish, add salt and black pepper, and stir until mixed.

4. Crack the egg in a bowl and then whisk it until blended.

5. Working on one avocado piece at a time, first dip it in the egg, then coat it in the almond flour mixture and place it on a wire rack.

6. Open the fryer, add avocado pieces to it in a single layer, spray oil over avocado, close with its lid and cook for

10 minutes until nicely golden and crispy, shaking halfway through the frying.

7. When the air fryer beeps, open its lid, transfer avocado fries onto a serving plate and serve.

Sandwich with Sliced Chicken/Turkey

Time required:
10 minutes

Servings: 01

INGREDIENTS

1 slice of sprouted wheat bread

1 tablespoon mustard

2 large lettuce leaves

2 slices of turkey or chicken without nitrates

a few slices of red onion tomato slices

sea salt and freshly ground pepper

STEPS FOR COOKING

1. Spread the bread with mustard, lay the lettuce leaves on top, and then the turkey or chicken slices. Add the onion and tomato.

2. Season with salt and pepper.

3. Serve.

Grilled Salmon

Time required:
20 minutes

Servings: 02

INGREDIENTS

1 lb. Salmon Fillet,
sliced into smaller
fillets

1 Lemon, large, and
sliced into rounds

1 tbsp. Avocado Oil

¼ tsp. Sea Salt

1 tbsp. Herbs De
Province or Italian
Seasoning

STEPS FOR COOKING

1. Preheat the grill to medium-high.
2. Keep the salmon fillets on a large foil sheet.
3. Spoon the avocado oil over it and brush it all over the fillets.
4. Add the Italian seasoning and sea salt over the fillets and coat them over it.
5. Top them with the lemon slices and wrap them in aluminum foil to make a foil packet.
6. Place them on the grill and cook them for 1o to 15 minutes or until the fish is cooked while keeping it covered.
7. Remove the fish from the grill and unwrap the foil when it is cool to handle.
8. Serve it hot.

Chicken with Coconut Sauce

Time required:
35 minutes

Servings: 02

INGREDIENTS

*1/2 lb. chicken
breasts*

1/3 cup red onion

*1 tbsp paprika
(smoked)*

2 tsp cornstarch

*1/2 cup light
coconut milk*

*1 tbsp extra virgin
olive oil*

2 tbsp fresh cilantro

*1 (10-oz) can
tomatoes and green
chilis*

1/4 cup water

STEPS FOR COOKING

1. Cut chicken into little cubes; sprinkle with 1,5 tsp paprika.
2. Heat oil, add chicken and cook for 3 to 5 minutes.
3. Remove from skillet, and fry the finely chopped onion for 5 minutes.
4. Return chicken to pan. Add tomatoes,1,5 tsp paprika, and water. Bring to a boil, and then simmer for 4 minutes.
5. Mix cornstarch and coconut milk; stir into the chicken mixture, and cook until it has done.
6. Sprinkle with chopped cilantro.

Cantaloupe and Prosciutto Salad

Time required:
15 minutes

Servings: 04

INGREDIENTS

6 mozzarella balls,
quartered

1 medium
cantaloupe, peeled
and cut into small
cubes

4 oz prosciutto,
chopped

1 tbsp. fresh lime
juice

1 tbsp. fresh mint,
chopped

2 tbsps. extra virgin
olive oil

1 tsp. honey

Salt and pepper to
taste

STEPS FOR COOKING

1. In a large bowl, whisk together oil,
    lime juice, honey, and mint, then
    season with salt and pepper to taste.
2. Add the cantaloupe and mozzarella
    and toss to combine. Arrange the
    mixture on a serving plate and add
    prosciutto.
3. Serve.

Curried Red Cauliflower Soup

Time required:
25 minutes

Servings: 04

INGREDIENTS

3 tablespoons of olive oil

1 large cauliflower in pieces

2 medium onions, diced

1 teaspoon of curry

1/2 teaspoon of pink Himalayan sea salt

1 tablespoon of lemon juice

4 cups of vegetable broth

3 cups unsweetened whole coconut milk

STEPS FOR COOKING

1. Let the oven preheat to 200°C.
2. Spread onions and cauliflower in a baking dish with parchment paper
3. Sprinkle olive oil evenly over the top and bake for 20 minutes.
4. When done cooking, whisk the onions and cauliflower with the vegetable broth.
5. In a saucepan over medium heat, pour the resulting smoothie and add the coconut milk, stir for 2 minutes.
6. Now add the curry, lemon juice, and pink salt, mix well for another minute. Serve hot.
7. Enjoy your meal!

Chicken Soup

Time required:
30 minutes

Servings: 06

INGREDIENTS

16 oz. Chicken, cooked and diced

6 cups Bone Broth

1 Bay Leaf, whole

¼ cup White Wine, dry

8 Oz. Celery Root, cubed

Salt and Pepper, as needed

½ of 1 Onion, diced

2 tsp. Chicken Bouillon

1/3 cup Carrot, roll cut

1 Garlic clove, large and sliced

STEPS FOR COOKING

1. In a pot over medium-high heat add butter.

2. Once the butter has melted, stir in all the vegetables, bay leaf, and lemon zest. Mix well.

3. Lower the heat and spoon in the garlic powder, chicken bouillon, and wine. Combine.

4. Cover the pot and cook for 4 minutes or until the vegetables are sweated bit not browned.

5. Pour the bone broth and bring the mixture to a boil.

6. Lower the heat and allow the mixture to simmer until the vegetables get cooked.

INGREDIENTS	STEPS FOR COOKING

1 tbsp. Garlic Powder

4 tbsp. Butter

1 cup Celery, sliced

1 tsp. Lemon Zest

7. When the vegetables become tender, add the chicken, salt, and pepper.

8. Serve it hot.

Fish with Fresh Herb Sauce

Time required:
20 minutes

Servings: 02

INGREDIENTS

2 (4-oz) cod fillets

1/3 cup fresh cilantro

1/4 tsp cumin

1 tbsp red onion

2 tsp extra virgin olive oil

1 tsp red wine vinegar

1 small clove garlic

1/8 tsp salt

1/8 black pepper

STEPS FOR COOKING

1. Combine chopped cilantro, finely chopped onion, oil, red wine vinegar, minced garlic, and salt, then sprinkle both sides of fish fillets with cumin and pepper.

2. Cook fillets 4 minutes per side.

3. Top each fillet with cilantro mixture.

Radish Chips

Time required:
25 minutes

Servings: 02

INGREDIENTS	STEPS FOR COOKING

INGREDIENTS

8 oz. radish slices
½ tsp. garlic powder
1 tsp. salt
½ tsp. onion powder
½ tsp. ground black pepper
Cooking spray

STEPS FOR COOKING

1. Wash the radish slices, pat them dry, place them in a fryer basket, and then spray oil on them until well coated.

2. Sprinkle salt, garlic powder, onion powder, and black pepper over radish slices and then toss until well coated.

3. Switch on the air fryer, insert fryer basket, then shut with its lid, set the fryer at 370°F, and cook for 10 minutes, stirring the slices halfway through.

4. Then spray oil on radish slices, shake the basket and continue frying for 10 minutes, stirring the chips halfway through.

5. Serve straight away.

Mushroom Pasta

Time required:
17 minutes

Servings: 04

INGREDIENTS

4 oz whole-grain linguine

1 tsp extra virgin olive oil

1/2 cup light sauce

2 tbsp green onion

1 (8-oz) pkg mushrooms

1 clove garlic

1/8 tsp salt

1/8 tsp pepper

STEPS FOR COOKING

1. Cook pasta according to package directions, drain.

2. Fry sliced mushrooms for 4 minutes.

3. Stir in fettuccine minced garlic, salt, and pepper. Cook 2 minutes.

4. Heat light sauce until heated; top pasta mixture properly with sauce and with finely-chopped green onion.

Avocado and Cauliflower Hummus

Time required:
35 minutes

___

Servings: 02

INGREDIENTS

1 large Hass avocado, peeled, pitted, and chopped

6 tablespoons of extra virgin olive oil

2 small garlic cloves

Half a tablespoon of lemon juice

Half teaspoon of onion powder

Halls

Black pepper (optional)

1 carrot

1/4 cup fresh cilantro, chopped

STEPS FOR COOKING

1. Preheat the oven to 220°C and line a baking sheet with aluminum foil.

2. Place chopped cauliflower on a baking sheet and drizzle with 2 tablespoons olive oil.

3. Bake the chopped cauliflower in the oven for 25 minutes

4. Remove the tray from the oven, then let it cool.

5. When the cauliflower starts to cool down, add along with it all the other ingredients inside a blender and run it!

6. Transfer the resulting mixture to a bowl, cover, and refrigerate for 45 minutes.

INGREDIENTS	STEPS FOR COOKING
	7. Remove the mixture from the fridge and season with salt and pepper.
	8. Enjoy your meal!

Zucchini Noodles with Pesto

Time required:
30 minutes

Servings: 04

INGREDIENTS

4 Zucchini, small, ends trimmed

¼ cup Parmesan Cheese, freshly grated

2 Garlic cloves

2 tsp. Lemon Juice, fresh

Salt and Pepper, as needed

2 cups Basil Leaves, fresh

1/3 cup Virgin Olive Oil

STEPS FOR COOKING

1. Slice the zucchini to noodles using a mandoline slicer or julienne peeler.
2. Place the basil and garlic in the food processor until chopped coarsely.
3. Slowly spoon the olive oil into the food processor while it is running.
4. Open the food processor and scrape the sides using a spatula.
5. To this, spoon in the lemon juice and parmesan cheese and pulse until mixed.
6. Add salt and pepper as needed.
7. Combine the zucchini and pesto in a large mixing bowl.
8. Serve and enjoy it.

Arizona Cactus and Beans

Time required:
33 minutes

Servings: 06

INGREDIENTS

2 tsp. vegetable oil

2 potatoes, cut into small rectangles

1 cup shredded carrots

2 1/2 (15-oz.) jars nopalitos, drained

1 tbsp. chili powder

2 garlic cloves, minced

2 tsp. fenugreek seeds

2 tsp. ground coriander

1/2 tsp. ground cumin

1 (15-oz.) can pinto beans

STEPS FOR COOKING

1. In a skillet, heat oil over moderate heat. Put in carrots and potatoes, then cook and stir for 10 minutes, until potatoes are softened.

2. Stir into the potato mixture with cumin, coriander, fenugreek seeds, garlic, chili powder, and nopalitos.

3. Cook for 5 minutes while stirring often, until nopalitos are tender.

4. Put in pinto beans and cook for 3 minutes while stirring gently until just heated through.

Tomato and Roasted Cod

Time required:
45 minutes

Servings: 02

INGREDIENTS	STEPS FOR COOKING

2 (4-oz) cod fillets

1 cup cherry tomatoes

2/3 cup onion

2 tsp orange rind

1 tbsp extra virgin olive oil

1 tsp thyme, dried

1/4 tsp salt, divided

1/4 tsp pepper, divided

1. Preheat oven to 400°F. Mix in half tomatoes, sliced onion, grated orange rind, extra virgin olive oil, dried thyme, and 1/8 salt and pepper. Fry 25 minutes. Remove from oven.

2. Arrange fish on pan, and flavor with remaining 1/8 tsp each salt and pepper. Put reserved tomato mixture over fish. Bake 10 minutes.

Tenderloin Grilled Salad

Time required:
30 minutes

Servings: 05

INGREDIENTS

1 lb. pork tenderloin

10 cups mixed salad greens

2 oranges, seedless, cut into bite-sized pieces

1 tablespoon orange zest, grated

2 tablespoons of cider vinegar

2 tablespoons olive oil

2 teaspoons Dijon mustard

2 teaspoons honey

1/2 teaspoon ground pepper

STEPS FOR COOKING

1. Bring together all the dressing ingredients in a bowl.
2. Grill each side of the pork covered over medium heat for 9 minutes.
3. Slice after 5 minutes.
4. Slice the tenderloin thinly.
5. Keep the greens on your serving plate.
6. Top with the pork and oranges.
7. Sprinkle nuts (optional).

Rice and Beans

Time required:
3 hours

Servings: 04

INGREDIENTS	STEPS FOR COOKING

2 packages of frozen cauliflower rice

2 cans of black soybeans

1/2 cup of peeled hemp seeds

1 cup of vegetable broth

5 tablespoons of olive oil

2 teaspoons of garlic powder

1 teaspoon of onion powder

1 teaspoon of cumin

1 teaspoon of chili powder

1. Mix all ingredients (except oregano) and simmer for 3 hours.

2. Next, stir in oregano and season with a side dish of your choice, and serve.

3. Enjoy your meal!

INGREDIENTS

1/2 teaspoon of cayenne powder

1 tablespoon of oregano

A side dish of your choice

STEPS FOR COOKING

Spinach Shrimp Salad

Time required:
20 minutes

Servings: 04

INGREDIENTS

1 lb. uncooked
shrimp, peeled and
deveined

2 tablespoons
parsley, minced

¾ cup halved cherry
tomatoes

1 medium lemon

4 cups baby spinach

2 tablespoons butter

3 minced garlic
cloves

¼ teaspoon pepper

¼ teaspoon salt

STEPS FOR COOKING

1. Melt the butter over the medium temperature in a nonstick skillet.
2. Add the shrimp.
3. Now cook the shrimp for 3 minutes until your shrimp becomes pink.
4. Add the parsley and garlic.
5. Cook for another minute. Take out from the heat.
6. Keep the spinach in your salad bowl.
7. Top with the shrimp mix and tomatoes.
8. Drizzle lemon juice on the salad.
9. Sprinkle pepper and salt.

Tomato and Chili Soup

Time required:
70 minutes

Servings: 03

INGREDIENTS

Half a teaspoon of black pepper

2 cups of vegetable broth

1 Garlic head

1/4 teaspoon of cayenne pepper

3 tablespoons of olive oil

1 Onion, diced

Half a teaspoon of ground paprika

1/4 cup chopped Parsley

2 red peppers cut into cubes

1/4 teaspoon of Salt

STEPS FOR COOKING

1. Heat the oven to 220°C.
2. Use a large bowl to mix tomatoes, red pepper, paprika, parsley, tomato puree, garlic and onion, pepper, salt, and olive oil.
3. Spread the peppers on a baking sheet greased with oil and bake for 45 minutes. Then pour over the mixture made in step 2.
4. Pour the broth into a pot and heat until boiling, lower the heat, add the pan's contents, stir well, and cook for 15 minutes.
5. Enjoy your meal!

INGREDIENTS

2 spoons of tomato
puree
3 diced tomatoes

STEPS FOR COOKING

Cauliflower Fried Rice

Time required:
25 minutes

Servings: 06

INGREDIENTS

1 Cauliflower, large

2 tbsp. Soy Sauce

2 tbsp. Butter

Salt and Pepper, to taste

½ of 1 Red Pepper, chopped

2 Eggs, large and lightly beaten

½ of 1 Green Pepper, chopped

2 tbsp. Sesame Oil, toasted

2 ½ tbsp. Ginger, fresh & grated

3 Scallions, chopped

1 tbsp. Garlic, chopped

STEPS FOR COOKING

1. Place the cauliflower florets in a food processor and process them for 1 to 2 minutes or until rice.

2. Heat a wok over medium-high heat and spoon in butter to it.

3. Once the butter gets melted, spoon in the ginger, garlic, and pepper along with the whites of the scallions. Saute for 3 minutes.

4. Stir in the cauliflower and cook for further 3 minutes while mixing it regularly.

5. Spoon the sauce and salt over it. Mix.

6. Place the rice to one side of the pan and stir in the whisked eggs.

7. Taste for seasoning and spoon in more salt and pepper to the eggs if needed.

INGREDIENTS	STEPS FOR COOKING
	8. Cook for a further one minute and combine it with the rest of the ingredients.
	9. Spoon the sesame oil and remove it from heat, then garnish with the green part of the onion.
	10. Serve and enjoy it.

Sage Beef

Time required:
40 minutes

Servings: 04

INGREDIENTS

2 lbs. beef stew meat, cubed

1 tbsp. sage, chopped

2 tbsps. butter, melted

½ tsp. coriander, ground

½ tbsp. garlic powder

1 tsp. Italian seasoning

Salt and black pepper to the taste

STEPS FOR COOKING

1. In the air fryer's pan, mix the beef with the sage, melted butter, and the other ingredients, introduce the pan to the fryer and cook at 360°F for 30 minutes.

2. Divide everything between plates and serve.

Potato Calico Salad

Time required:
20 minutes

Servings: 14

INGREDIENTS

4 red potatoes, peeled and cooked

1-1/2 cups kernel corn, cooked

1/2 cup green pepper, diced

1/2 cup red onion, chopped

1 cup carrot, shredded

1/2 cup olive oil

¼ cup vinegar

1-1/2 teaspoons chili powder

1 teaspoon salt

STEPS FOR COOKING

1. Keep all the ingredients together in a jar.
2. Close it and shake well.
3. Cube the potatoes. Combine with the carrot, onion, and corn in your salad bowl.
4. Pour the dressing over.
5. Now toss lightly.

Zucchini Casserole

Time required:
25 minutes

Servings: 02

INGREDIENTS

4 zucchini cut into slices

120 g of butter cut into cubes

1 sliced onion

1/4 cup grated parmesan cheese

Halls

Pepper

STEPS FOR COOKING

1. In a casserole dish, layer zucchini slices, onion, butter, pepper, and salt and put grated Parmesan cheese on top

2. Cover the casserole dish with parchment paper and bake in a 175°C oven for 45 minutes.

3. Enjoy your meal!

Cauliflower Pizza

Time required:
30 minutes

Servings: 08

INGREDIENTS	STEPS FOR COOKING

INGREDIENTS

1 Cauliflower head, medium

½ tsp. Basil

¼ cup Parmesan Cheese, shredded

1 Egg

1 cup Marinara Sauce

¼ cup Mozzarella Cheese

¼ tsp. Salt

½ tsp. Oregano, minced

½ tsp. Garlic Powder

STEPS FOR COOKING

1. Preheat the oven to 500° F.
2. Place the cauliflower florets in a food processor and pulse the cauliflower until it gets a riced texture.
3. Microwave the riced cauliflower in a safe microwave bowl for 5 minutes on high power.
4. Allow the riced cauliflower to cool for at least 5 to 10 minutes.
5. Once the cauliflower is cooled, place it in a cheesecloth and squeeze out all the water as much as possible.
6. Mix the cauliflower, garlic, cheese, egg, and seasoning until you get a dough-like texture.
7. Place the cauliflower dough onto a greased parchment paper-lined pizza pan.

INGREDIENTS	STEPS FOR COOKING

8. Bake it for 13 to 15 minutes or until the crust is golden and crusty.

9. Top it with the marinara sauce and mozzarella cheese and return to the oven.

10. Turn on the broiler function of the oven and bake for 2 to 3 minutes or until the cheese is gooey.

11. Serve it hot.

Strawberry Salsa

Time required:
15 minutes

Servings: 04

INGREDIENTS

4 tomatoes, seeded and chopped

1-pint strawberry, chopped

1 red onion, chopped

2 tablespoons of juice from a lime

1 jalapeno pepper, minced

1 tablespoon olive oil

2 garlic cloves, minced

STEPS FOR COOKING

1. Bring together the strawberries, tomatoes, jalapeno, and onion in the bowl.
2. Stir in the garlic, oil, and lime juice.
3. Refrigerate. Serve with separately cooked pork or poultry.

Cheese and Eggplant Casserole

Time required:
35 minutes

Servings: 02

INGREDIENTS

2 eggplants

2 tablespoons of olive oil

1 and a half cups of mozzarella cut into small pieces

1 ½ cups marinara sauce

Half a cup of parmesan cheese

Salt to taste

1 medium tomato cut into slices

Optional: black pepper

Optional: Chopped fresh basil

STEPS FOR COOKING

1. Preheat the oven to 175°C and line the baking sheet with baking paper greased with 1 tablespoon of olive oil.

2. Cut the eggplant into thin slices and sprinkle a little salt on top, then transfer them to the greased baking dish.

3. Bake for 8 minutes (4 minutes per side).

4. Remove the pan from the oven, then set it aside. Do not turn off the oven!

5. Take another baking sheet and grease it with the other tablespoon of olive oil.

6. Add the layer of eggplant slices (prepared in step 3), then pour the sauce, a few slices of tomato, parmesan cheese, and mozzarella.

INGREDIENTS	STEPS FOR COOKING
	7. Repeat until the pan is filled with the different layers.
	8. Finally, bake the completed pan with all layers in the oven for 20 minutes.
	9. Enjoy your meal!

Pumpkin Soup

Time required:
40 minutes

Servings: 03

INGREDIENTS	STEPS FOR COOKING

INGREDIENTS

1 ½ Vegetable Broth

1/8 tsp. Nutmeg

1 cup Pumpkin Puree

3 tbsp. Bacon Grease

4 tbsp. Butter

½ cup Heavy Whipping Cream

¼ of 1 Onion, medium and chopped

1 Bay Leaf, large

2 Garlic cloves, roasted and minced

¼ tsp. Cinnamon

STEPS FOR COOKING

1. Melt butter in a large saucepan over medium-low heat, then once the butter is dark-golden brown color, stir in the onions, ginger, and garlic to the pan.

2. Saute for 3 minutes and then spoon in the spices. Combine and cook for further 2 minutes.

3. Pour the vegetable broth and pumpkin puree into the pan. Mix.

4. Bring the soup to a simmer for 20 minutes after lowering the heat. Remove from heat.

5. Transfer the mixture to an immersion blender or blender once slightly cooled.

6. Blend the soup until it is completely smooth and pureed.

INGREDIENTS

½ tsp. Salt and
Pepper
¼ tsp. Coriander
½ tsp. Ginger, fresh
and minced

STEPS FOR COOKING

7. Return the soup to the pan and cook for another 20 minutes.

8. Pour the cream and bacon grease into it.

9. Serve hot.

Tabasco Shrimp

Time required:
15 minutes

Servings: 04

INGREDIENTS	STEPS FOR COOKING

INGREDIENTS

1 lb. big shrimp, peeled and deveined

1 tsp. cayenne pepper

2 tbsps. butter melted

1 tsp. Tabasco sauce

Salt and black pepper to the taste

1 tbsp. parsley, chopped

STEPS FOR COOKING

1. In your air fryer, combine the shrimp with the cayenne, butter, and the other ingredients, toss and cook at 370°F for 10 minutes.

2. Divide into bowls and serve right away.

Tomato Toasts

Time required:
10 minutes

Servings: 04

INGREDIENTS	STEPS FOR COOKING

4 slices of sprouted bread toast

2 tomatoes, sliced

1 avocado, mashed

1 teaspoon olive oil

1 pinch of salt

¾ teaspoon ground black pepper

1. Blend together the olive oil, mashed avocado, salt, and ground black pepper.
2. When the mixture is homogenous – spread it over the sprouted bread.
3. Then place the sliced tomatoes over the toasts.
4. Enjoy!

Key Lime Pie

Time required:
35 minutes

Servings: 16

INGREDIENTS

For the Base:

3 oz. Butter melted

7 oz. Almond Meal

1 tbsp. Swerve

¼ cup Golden Flax Meal

For the Filling:

Zest of 3 Limes

½ cup Heavy Cream

4 Eggs

½ cup Key Lime Juice

14 oz. Condensed Milk, sugar-free

For Topping:

7 fl. oz. Heavy Cream

STEPS FOR COOKING

1. Preheat the oven to 340° F.
2. Mix almond meal, swerve, and flax meal in a large mixing bowl until combined.
3. Spoon in the melted butter and stir.
4. Transfer the mixture to a greased springform pan and press it slightly down and up the sides.
5. Bake for 12 minutes. Allow it to cool.
6. To make the filling:
7. Lower the temperature to 300°F.
8. Whisk egg and condensed milk in another bowl at medium speed and slowly lower the speed.
9. Pour the lime juice slowly into it, followed by cream and lime zest.

INGREDIENTS	STEPS FOR COOKING
	10. Transfer the mixture onto the top of the crust and bake for further 40 minutes or until just set in the center.
	11. Allow it to cool for 20 minutes and then place in the refrigerator for 2 hours.
	12. Whip the cream and spread.
	13. Serve and enjoy.

Peanut Butter Banana "Ice Cream"

Time required:
10 minutes

Servings: 06

INGREDIENTS	STEPS FOR COOKING

4 medium bananas
½ cup whipped
peanut butter
1 tsp. vanilla extract

1. Peel the bananas, then slice them into coins.
2. Arrange the slices on a plate and freeze until solid, then place the frozen bananas in a food processor.
3. Add the peanut butter and blend until it is mostly smooth.
4. Scrape down the sides, then add the vanilla extract.
5. Pulse until smooth, then spoon into bowls to serve.

Shortbread Cookies

Time required:
80 minutes

Servings: 06

INGREDIENTS

2 1/2 cups almond flour

6 tablespoons nut butter

1/2 cup erythritol

1 teaspoon vanilla essence

STEPS FOR COOKING

1. Preheat your oven to 350 degrees F.
2. Layer a cookie sheet with parchment paper.
3. Beat butter with erythritol until fluffy.
4. Stir in vanilla essence and almond flour. Mix well until becomes crumbly.
5. Spoon out a tablespoon of cookie dough onto the cookie sheet, then add more dough to make as many cookies.
6. Bake for 15 minutes until brown.
7. Serve.

Strawberry Popsicles

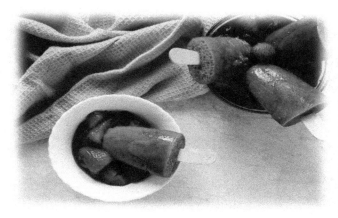

Time required:
5 minutes

Servings: 06

INGREDIENTS

*5 drops of Liquid
Stevia*

*¼ cup Oats, old-
fashioned, grounded*

*4 oz. Cottage
Cheese, low-fat*

Juice from 4 Lemons

1 ½ lb. Strawberries

STEPS FOR COOKING

1. Add all the ingredients to a high-speed blender and blend until it becomes smooth.

2. Once pureed, pour the mixture into the popsicle molds and place it in the freezer overnight or for a minimum of 6 hours.

3. Serve and enjoy.

Mini Apple Oat Muffins

Time required:
30 minutes

Servings: 24

INGREDIENTS	STEPS FOR COOKING

INGREDIENTS

1 ½ cups old-fashioned oats

1 tsp. baking powder

½ tsp. ground cinnamon

¼ tsp. baking soda

¼ tsp. salt

½ cup unsweetened applesauce

¼ cup light brown sugar

3 tbsps. canola oil

3 tbsps. water

1 tsp. vanilla extract

½ cup slivered almonds

STEPS FOR COOKING

1. Preheat the oven to 350°F and grease a mini muffin pan, then place the oats in a food processor and pulse into a fine flour.

2. Add the baking powder, cinnamon, baking soda, and salt.

3. Pulse until well combined, then add the applesauce, brown sugar, canola oil, water, and vanilla, then blend smooth.

4. Fold in the almonds and spoon the mixture into the muffin pan.

5. Bake for 25 minutes until cooked.

6. Cool the muffins for 5 minutes, then turn them out onto a wire rack.

Chocolate Mousse

Time required:
15 minutes

Servings: 04

INGREDIENTS

1/4 cup Cocoa
Powder,
unsweetened

1 cup Heavy
Whipping Cream

1 tsp. Vanilla Extract

¼ cup Low-Carb
Sweetener,
powdered

¼ tsp. Salt

STEPS FOR COOKING

1. Place the whipping cream in a large mixing bowl and whisk it with a mixer until you get stiff peaks.

2. Stir in the remaining ingredients and whisk until everything comes together.

3. Serve and enjoy.

Broiled Grapefruit

Time required:
10 minutes

Servings: 04

INGREDIENTS	STEPS FOR COOKING
2 Grapefruit, halved	1. Preheat the broiler.
Strawberries, as needed	2. Place the halved grapefruit on a baking sheet.
1 tbsp. Low-carb sweetener syrup of your choice	3. Spoon the sweetener syrup over each of the halved fruit and dust it with the grounded cinnamon.
¼ tsp. Cinnamon, grounded and as needed	4. Broil the grapefruit for 6 minutes or until slightly browned.
	5. Serve and enjoy.

Cinnamon Spiced Popcorn

Time required:
15 minutes

Servings: 04

INGREDIENTS

8 cups air-popped corn

2 tsp. sugar

½ to 1 tsp. ground cinnamon

Butter-flavored cooking spray

STEPS FOR COOKING

1. Preheat the oven to 350°F and line a shallow roasting pan with foil.
2. Pop the popcorn using your preferred method.
3. Spread the popcorn in the roasting pan and mix the sugar and cinnamon in a small bowl.
4. Lightly spray the popcorn with cooking spray and toss to coat evenly.
5. Sprinkle with cinnamon and toss again.
6. Bake for 5 minutes until just crisp, then serve warm.

Lemon Custard

Time required:
10 minutes

Servings: 04

INGREDIENTS

2 cups whipping cream or coconut cream

5 egg yolks

1 tablespoon lemon zest

1 teaspoon vanilla extract

1/4 cup fresh lemon juice, squeezed

1/2 teaspoon liquid stevia

Lightly sweetened whipped cream

STEPS FOR COOKING

1. Whisk egg yolks together with lemon zest, liquid stevia, lemon zest, and vanilla in a bowl, and then whisk in heavy cream.

2. Divide the mixture among 4 small jars or ramekins.

3. To the bottom of a slow cooker add a rack, and then add ramekins on top of the rack and add enough water to cover half of the ramekins.

4. Close the lid and cook for 3 hours on low. Remove ramekins.

5. Let cool to room temperature, and then place into the refrigerator to cool completely for about 3 hours.

6. When through, top with the whipped cream and serve. Enjoy!

Blueberry Muffins

Time required:
40 minutes

Servings: 03

INGREDIENTS	STEPS FOR COOKING

INGREDIENTS

1/2 cup of Blueberries

3/4 cup of Teff Flour

3/4 cup of Spelt Flour

1/3 cup of Agave Syrup

1/2 teaspoon of Pure Sea Salt

1 cup of Coconut Milk

1/4 cup of Sea Moss Gel (optional, check information)

Grape Seed Oil

STEPS FOR COOKING

1. Preheat your oven to 365 degrees Fahrenheit.

2. Grease or line 6 standard muffin cups.

3. Add Teff, Spelt flour, Pure Sea Salt, Coconut Milk, Sea Moss Gel, and Agave Syrup to a large bowl, then mix them together.

4. Add Blueberries to the mixture and mix well.

5. Divide muffin batter among the 6 muffin cups.

6. Bake for 30 minutes until golden brown.

7. Serve and enjoy your Blueberry Muffins!

CPSIA information can be obtained
at www.ICGtesting.com
Printed in the USA
BVHW090305050621
608821BV00011B/2458

9 781802 611007